How to Live With A

GOLFAHOLIC

A Survival Guide for Family and Friends of Passionate Players

Mark Oman

Illustrated By Jay Campbell & Carl Christ

A Golfaholics Anonymous Book™

Published by Golfaholics Anonymous®
P.O. Box 222357
Carmel, CA 93922

Library of Congress Catalog Card Number: 87-81273
International Standard Book Number: 0-917346-14-9

Printed in the United States of America

This book is dedicated to all those people who have put up with a golf lover's magnificent obsession—without going O.B. themselves.

Your cries have been heard...

Your prayers are about to be answered!

WARNING!

The following is intended solely for the private use of those who suspect they may be friends of, related to, or — heaven forbid — married to a golfaholic.

What you are about to read may be the most important *therapy* for your passionate player's handicap since admitting he had one!

TABLE OF CONTENTS

Fore-word!
THE ADDICTION DOCTORS DON'T
WANT YOU TO KNOW ABOUT...

PART I
THE GREAT SOCIAL DISEASE
OF THE 80's!
(And higher — depending on the
magnitude of one's handicap)

PART II
SURVIVAL OF THE FITTEST!

THE UNREACHABLE PAR

**...ACUTE BALL-BEATING DEPENDENCY HAS SPREAD
THROUGH EVERY SECTOR OF THE MEDICAL WORLD**

THE ADDICTION DOCTORS DON'T WANT YOU TO KNOW ABOUT...

Absolutely true! And the coverup doesn't stop there. Why even the church is keeping buttoned up about it. Ask your clergyman about the hellish nature of golf and he'll just smile, then pray for a good lie from the Pro upstairs.

But the medical profession is even worse! No one will give you a straight answer. In fact, the entire medical profession would just as soon forget they had ever heard the word.

Golfaholism.

That's right, golfaholism! An addiction obviously deserving of a place on every psychiatrist's couch. Then why isn't it there? Why aren't its practitioners there?

Even more important, why does the medical professional act as though the word doesn't exist?

I'll tell you why. Because doctors are the most shameless golfaholics of all!! That's why.

7

There is now overwhelming evidence to suggest that *"acute ball-beating dependency"* has spread through every sector of the medical world. It certainly is no secret that surgeons, technicians, chiropractors, radio talk show therapists and the like have all been subjected to peer group pressure to regularly engage in mid-week *"fixes."*

Statistics prove beyond a doubt that as a group, doctors more than anyone else, are willing to pay the price for *"lost weekends"* at La Costa and Pebble Beach.

Let's face it. The medical profession is rampant with hard-core overheated swingers! Did you ever doubt it? It is not surprising they don't want to talk about it. They don't dare. Before they could possibly help others, they would have to help themselves. Look at themselves in the mirror and face the truth:

- **That they would rather pay the price for a bad slice in the O.R. than pay the penalty for slicing it O.B. on the course.**
- **That giving a new heart to a human being may be very satisfying...But cutting the sandbagger's heart out on the golf course is what really makes their day!**
- **That the healing profession is as honorable and meaningful a career as anyone could hope to dedicate their life to...**

But they would sell their stethoscope, scalpel and stirrups, and hock their Hippocratic oath if they could swing like *"The Golden Bear,"* crunch the ball like the *"Great White Shark,"* putt like *"Gentle Ben,"* hitch their pants like *"The King,"* and beat the young, blonde, flat-belly pro at their club.

Now that is the truth! We all know it. And they do too.

So what is the bottom line, net score?

Not until the medical profession has found a way to rid themselves of their mounting handicap (or at least reduce it to a respectable single digit level) will they speak out to raise the public consciousness about this epidemic running amok across America!

You don't believe me?

Ask your family G.P. He won't have time to talk to you. He's off to the golf course for a healthy dose of self-abuse.

Don't expect any help from your local hospital either. You will find no treatment centers for *putter paranoia.*

The U.C.L.A. Medical Center is not conducting lab tests on the long term after-affects of *bogey binging!*

The fact is no one has dared to step forward, to *"come out of the locker room"* and tell you the truth...

Until now.

9

"Give me golf clubs, the fresh air, and a beautiful partner and you can keep my golf clubs and the fresh air."

JACK BENNY

"Give me golf clubs, the fresh air, and a beautiful partner...and she better be able to putt!"

ANONYMOUS GOLFAHOLIC

PART I:

THE GREAT
SOCIAL DISEASE OF THE 80's!
(And higher—depending on the
magnitude of one's handicap)

In the following pages you'll learn the whole sordid story; how to survive the traps and hazards of life with a golf ball junkie.

GOLFAHOLISM...

The Word Itself Is Enough To Give Some Swingers The "Yips"

But we can't be afraid to talk about it. The only way to deal with the condition and its practitioners is to confront it and them head on! (Preferably from the rear—about the only safe place to stand the way most golfaholics attack the ball.)

So let's look at the word from all sides; find out what it really means.

GOLF-A-HOL-ISM—A depraved manifestation of various types of self-abuse, wherein practitioners use clubs of wood and iron to inflict pain and pleasure on themselves and others of their ilk.

Then how did it get a reputation as just a silly game *"whose aim is to hit a very small ball into an even smaller hole with weapons singularly ill-designed for the purpose,"* as Sir Winston Churchill is reported to have said.

And what about those non-addicts who regard golf as nothing more than *"a lot of walking broken up by disappointment and bad arithmetic"*—a definition not entirely without merit. This is usually the same camp which holds that golf is *"a game where the ball invariably lies poorly, and the golfer well!"*

Of course there are many who simply think of golf as a four letter word more meaningful spelled backwards: Flog. Which fairly well describes how most of its addictees play it forwards!

However you choose to define it, the addiction to golf is not new. In fact, shortly after it was invented, it became quite clear that the game was beginning to have a strange hold over those who played it.

When the game became more important than archery practice, the Scottish Parliament of King James II in 1457 issued a proclamation: *"Golfe be utterly cryed down and not be used."*

A hundred and fifty years later Parliament loosened up a bit forbidding golf only during Sunday hours of *"devine services."* Obviously, politicians were now hooked.

And today?

We play every day, all day and into the night! There aren't enough days in the week to satisfy the golfing appetites of millions of devout swingers.

We are willing to sacrifice work, friendship, marriage, mental stability and our emotional well-being if there is any hope of gaining the favor of the golfing gods. We mumble silent prayers and unholy promises in hopes they'll be forgiving when we stray from their divine fairways and merciful towards our pitiful offerings on the greenswards of their 18 holy places of worship.

You may ask how it is this writer knows so well the intoxicating hold the game has on its most committed and devout followers.

The answer will be painfully obvious in a moment.

**FROM ITS EARLIEST BEGINNINGS GOLF HAD A
STRANGE HOLD OVER THOSE WHO PLAYED IT**

CASE HISTORIES

Throughout this book you will find Case Histories of real golfaholics. By showing you the behavior of these die-hard golf junkies—as described by themselves and their loved ones—you should be able to get a much better sense of the magnitude of your own golfer's lust for the links.

The Case Histories included are not unique, but everyday examples of the kinds of behavior engaged in by millions of people hopelessly bewitched, bothered and bogey-brained by this thing called golf.

Yes, these stories are true. But our subjects must remain anonymous—to protect innocent friends and families.

To answer those skeptics who may think this book is a case of the pot calling the kettle black, the following confession is offered...

CONFESSIONS OF A GOLF JUNKIE

Yes, this writer is a golfaholic.

It began in earnest in 1957. I'd close the door to my room and watch *"All Star Golf"* on the television while fondling and cleaning my first set of clubs. Of course I was still a virgin. Hadn't even abused my putter. What did I know? I was only 14.

I have to admit that a great deal of the intoxication of the game was that you could do it alone. It made me feel grown up. All I needed was Joe Kirkwood's 9 Hole Pitch 'n Putt Golf Course and Driving Range near my home in Studio City, California, to learn how to become an experienced swinger—a man!

The golf course and driving range were regularly patronized by an unusually high concentration of movie actors, producers and writers living in the area—a veritable den of depravity.

The small pro shop was always full of enticing new golf paraphernalia. I experimented with it all, ravenously.

It was all very seductive to an impressionable young man such as I.

Convincing my mother that golf was a gentleman's sport of fair play and rational behavior was easily accomplished since no one in my mother's family had ever played the game.

(Born and raised in Southern California my parents were naturally divorced at an early age—theirs and mine—so my father was not a real factor in my golf attraction. Nor were my stepfathers. In truth, my mother was married so many times that on Father's Day I had to leave town! But that's another book.)

So unaware of the hazards lurking just ahead, mother encouraged my interest and I began lessons!

Whether the pro at the driving range had a keen eye for raw talent or just a keen eye for my mother watching my lessons, I wasn't sure at the time. Looking back it must have been mom. It certainly wasn't my golfing talent. Nevertheless, that pro did give me my first pair of real, all leather professional golf shoes.

That was nearly 30 years ago. And while I no longer wear them, I often pull them out and harken back to old times. In fact, just having them around gives me a sense of inner peace.

LOOKING GOOD!

Anyway, it wasn't long after those first lessons and hanging around the driving range that my interest turned into an anxiousness about the game and eventually into deep dependency.

The moment I had my driver's license I'd sneak out at night and find out-of-the-way driving ranges where I'd *"shoot up"* with 2 or 3 or often 4 buckets of balls!

Of course from there I couldn't help going *"all the way"* spending every penny I could scrounge to experience the thrills of the *"hard stuff"* like Torrey Pines South Course. From the blue tees. Thirty-six holes!

I began socializing with other addicts and together we'd *"trip out"* to Monterey and let it all hang out at Spyglass Hill and Pebble Beach. I'm talking hard-core ball-beating. Equipment abuse! The whole nine yards!

Where did all this get me?

Eventually to the understanding that my life and golf were inextricably bound together. This self realization didn't really take hold until about 10 years ago when I found that my marriage was in trouble because of my shameless golfaholic appetites. I came to realize that there was a real correlation between my handicap on the course during the day and my handicap under the covers later that night with my wife.

It took a real coming to grips with my golfaholic compulsion, facing the *unplayable lies* I had gotten myself into, to make me see clearly what I had to do. My search began.

From the Halls of St. Andrews to the Shores of Pebble Beach, I journeyed to find the answers to what turns normal folks, good people, into raving, wild-eyed, foaming at the ball washer golf animals.

Above all I found out that *not* talking about it, *not* owning up to our insatiable lust for the game, keeping it bottled up inside (save for the 19th hole), is *not* the answer!

"What is?" you ask.

Not so fast. You're not quite ready. First you have to understand how golfaholics got that way.

To find out, turn the page...

CASE HISTORY NO. 09600002
Cleveland, Ohio

"It all started on our wedding day. He was 10 minutes late to the ceremony because he felt he should probably take a shower after playing 36 holes of golf.

"After we were married, it was 36 holes on Saturday and 36 holes on Sunday. I finally put my foot down and insisted that if he played golf on Saturday, he had to spend time with the family on Sunday.

"He agreed. Now on Sunday the 3 year old and I walk around the course with him.

"Lately his handicap in bed has been going up faster than at the course.

"When I told him that, he said he really does want to have another child. But he's got to get his clubs reshafted first.

"When I suggested maybe it was time he saw a sex therapist, he agreed, but wanted to know the doctor's handicap first."

How GOLFAHOLICS GOT THAT WAY

What makes some players compulsive ball-beaters while others never seem to get past social swinging?

What is it about that dimpled little ball that drives ordinary people bananas?

Tough questions. But I think the closest to the truth is that for many of us golf is like a wild, passionate love affair. If you don't take it seriously, it's no fun. Of course, if you do take it seriously, it'll break your heart!

Now, it's not that golfaholics like to have their hearts broken every time they tee it up...but it is also the nature of the addiction that real golfaholics are not afraid to let it all hang out. To go for it. To put it on the line. Swing from the heels. To risk the thrill of victory and the agony of a lost ball!

I think it is because golfaholics tend to be truly passionate about all the finer things in life.

We love great golf courses, the finest food, generous libations, breathtaking sex...all in the course of one round when possible.

All right. So how did we get this way? When did it happen?

After years of research there seems to be little doubt that golfaholism is a *progressive addiction.*

It usually takes hold at a very early age, though there are some who avoid the virus until well into mid-life. I know what you are thinking, so let me get it over with right now.

Yes, it is almost always hereditary.

And the next most asked question: Is it contagious?

Again, yes. In fact, it is flagrantly contagious in the worst possible way. Direct contact is not even necessary to plant the ball-beating urge.

Television. There's the culprit!

YES, IT IS ALMOST ALWAYS HEREDITARY

CASE HISTORY NO. 732659
Hackensack, New Jersey

"I think I'm in trouble.

"Last month my boyfriend played in a Pro-Am with neck spasms, a wrenched back, two tennis elbows, water on the knee, and sunburned feet...(Don't ask!).

"Unfortunately he played the best game of his life. Now he refuses to play in any tournament unless he's a physical wreck and in major pain.

"He said if I really loved him, I'd help him get 'in shape' for the club championship next month. I did my best...

"Looks like he'll be out of the hospital just in time to tee it up!"

THE STUFF OF LEGENDS!

You have to realize that golfaholics see themselves as being different from ordinary golfers. Real golfaholics tend to march to a different drummer. They can be incredibly fearless in their quest to conquer the game.

Take, for example, the Battle of Britain. World War II, you remember. These were hard times, particularly for golfers. To meet the conditions, certain rules were written and adopted by the St. Mellon's Golf and Country Club. I think it is safe to say it took a golfaholic of the stiffest upper lip to play under the following conditions and rules:

1. **In competitions, during gunfire and while bombs are falling, players may take cover without penalty.**
2. **The positions of known delayed-action bombs are marked by red and white flags placed at reasonably, but not guaranteed, safe distances from the bombs.**
3. **A player whose stroke is affected by the explosion of a bomb or shell or by machine-gun fire, may play another ball from the same place, penalty— one stroke.**

With rules like that the 19th hole probably did a hell of a lot more business than the previous 18.

Todays die-hard golf lover fancies himself a somewhat different breed of character. More of a renegade from the ordinary, a maverick out of the masses.

These people tend to exude the traits of the legendary gamblers and gunfighters of the Old West.

They know when to hold 'em, know when to fold 'em...Know when to speak their mind...And when to let their putters do the talkin'.

The game itself promotes this kind of self image with its *"sudden death"* play-offs.

Watch Nicklaus, Palmer, or Norman, that fast gun from Australia, come striding up the 18th fairway and it's Gary Cooper, John Wayne, and Clint Eastwood marching up Main Street in Dodge City ready for the showdown!

We're talking the stuff of legends. Shootout at the OK Corral Golf Resort with blazing 6-irons!

SHOOTOUT WITH BLAZING 6-IRONS!

CASE HISTORY NO. 36721897
San Diego, California

"It's my father. He plays golf every day. On Saturday and Sunday he is part of the 'Dawn Patrol.'

"On Monday he plays with a bunch of 'bandits' at a local course.

"On Tuesday he plays with some other addicts. They go across the boarder to play in Mexico.

"On Wednesday he plays with another gang.

"On Thursday he plays with his own bunch of retired sandbaggers.

"And on Friday he likes to practice.

"He once told me 'golf is better than sex.'

"I asked my mother about that and she admitted I was adopted."

Warning Signs of the Addiction

All right. So, how do you know if someone you care about is really a golfaholic? What are the warning signs of the addiction you should be on the lookout for?

The following will help you zero in on those golfers with a high risk factor.

(NOTE: For consistency of terminology and clarity, we are using the masculine pronoun throughout this text. This by no means suggests we are ignoring the ever growing number of women golfaholics. To be sure, the female golfer can turn into a golfaholic of hair-raising proportions!)

If someone at your work place regularly takes four hour lunch breaks and tells you he has to go make a *"survey in turf management,"* you may be working for a golfaholic.

If you work in a high tech company, you will probably just get an inter-office memo saying something like:

"Must complete an empirical analysis into the aerodynamic properties and trajectories of an impelled non-oblatious alveolate spheroid.

"Upon completion of collection of data, a dissertation-review seminar will be conducted at the 19th interation where lubrication for research personnel will be available and grand funds et al. will be distributed...

"P.S. Tell my wife to start the tofu casserole without me."

Obviously this executive needs to have his headcovers examined.

There are certain words that trigger unconscious reactions in hard-core golfaholics.

Perhaps you're showing pictures of your children to a friend or next door neighbor and you say, *"Look at those cheeks. Have you ever seen such dimples!"*

"Dimples! You call those dimples??? I've got balls with dimples that'll make--"

You get the idea. Of course such a response is a dead giveaway. But the golfaholic can't help himself.

The golfer begins to believe that the longer he takes to address the ball, test the wind, barometric pressure and soil moisture, the better he's going to hit it.

But he's not really dedicated until he starts being extra careful lining up his fourth putt for a smooth 8 on a par 3.

While it is certainly better to know the truth about ones spouse before marriage, many people don't find out until it is almost too late.

Your fiance comes to you with an assortment of resort brochures and says *you* can pick where to go on your honeymoon.

You can't believe such thoughtfulness, until you discover the resorts are all conducting golf clinics that week.

On the other hand, if your betrothed wasn't quite so obvious, you may not discover the cold truth until the honeymoon itself.

You are in a luxurious, romantic paradise. The fact that your handsome, hard-bodied husband can't wait to rip off his clothes—instead of yours—put on his plaid knickers, grab his spikes and race to the first tee, is only mildly upsetting.

At least with him away you will have time to rest up from the long plane trip and prepare for your first night as man and wife.

It is after dark when the man you pledged to love, honor and cherish returns to your honeymoon suite.

You are ready for him. You look like Bo Derek, Linda Evans, and Diane Keaton rolled into one.

He looks like Buster Keaton. He has been humiliated by the course, betrayed by his clubs, and laughed at by his 12 year old caddie. He is physically and emotionally exhausted, wrung out, battered and bruised.

After a couple of hours of spilling his guts about every shot on every hole, he suddenly doesn't want to talk about it anymore. He wants to forget the whole thing.

"Good," you agree. Especially since it is now 9 P.M. You suggest he slip into something less color-coordinated and you will go to dinner.

You arrive at the restaurant looking ravishing and receive admiring glances from Tom Selleck at the bar.

This is obviously a 4-Star establishment.

Too bad your beloved is behaving like a 5-Star putz.

He glares glassy-eyed into his soup, dropping in crouton after crouton—another water hazard to dump balls into.

He picks at his salad, heart sick over the greens that got away.

He's lost his appetite.

You try to arouse a new one. You caress your carrots, devour the succulent flesh of your lobster, seduce your chocolate souffle...

He *"tops"* his sirloin, *"bogeys"* his baked potato, and *"shanks"* his sherbert *"out of bounds"* into his lap.

He has a headache and wants to leave.

Back at the room his mind is still reeling. He sheds his clothes and crawls under the warm and protecting covers.

You come out of the powder room in your Frederick's of Hollywood hot pajamas. The man you have chosen as your one and only is dead to the world asleep.

You've had it. You grab your lover's balls, clubs, and bag and put them where they belong—in bed with him.

You sit in a chair watching as your darkest fears come to light.

Your husband snuggles into the soft belly of his leather bag, droops a comforting arm around the head of his putter and sighs in blissful surrender.

All is forgiven. *By him!*

The next day the weather turns dark and nasty. You turn bright and hopeful! You are willing to forgive and forget, particularly when the wind and rain become so fierce that the two of you will have to stay inside all day. Together. Alone.

Sweet victory is about to be yours. Your husband seems ready to forget his backswing and concentrate on yours!

He's ready all right. To forget the honeymoon!

If he can't play golf and has to stay inside, what the hell are the two of you supposed to do all day?

After all, what's a honeymoon without golf??

Now if any of the above hits uncomfortably close to home, read on...

The worst is yet to come!

WHAT'S A HONEYMOON WITHOUT GOLF??

A TEST FOR POSITIVE IDENTIFICATION

We can't beat around the bush any longer. At some point you have to answer the hard questions about that special golfer in your life.

For many of you this is going to be painful. But you know you have to do it. If it makes it any easier, take this test in the privacy of your bedroom. Close the door. Only you will know the results.

Just try to answer the following questions as honestly as you can. There are no right or wrong answers. Only truths you may not have wished to accept.

THE FRONT 9

1. Does someone near and dear to you think about golf all the time? At the breakfast table does he say, "Please pass the putter?"

☐ **YES**   ☐ **NO**

2. Is there a divot in the carpet in front of the television in the den or family room?

☐ **YES**   ☐ **NO**

3. Does that special someone in your life put his name, telephone, and company on a golf ball instead of a business card?

☐ **YES**   ☐ **NO**

4. Does your spouse often engage in unconscious repetitious acts like wiggling his feet, waggling his rear and hitching up his pants?

☐ **YES**   ☐ **NO**

5. Does he practice his grip, stance, or swing naked in the bathroom, outside church, on airplanes, or in other public places?

☐ **YES**   ☐ **NO**

6. Have you ever gone shopping and turned around to find him standing in front of a full-length mirror taking a full swing at a ball that isn't there with a club that isn't there?

☐ **YES**   ☐ **NO**

7. Has the love of your life turned into a golfing mailman? In other words, neither rain, nor snow, nor dark of night keep him from his appointed rounds?

☐ **YES**   ☐ **NO**

8. Does his nose twitch when he gets within 1,760 yards of a golf course? (To any normal person that's one mile. To a golfaholic, it's 1,760 yards to the first tee!)

☐ **YES**   ☐ **NO**

9. Does his passionate pursuit of the game know no bounds...like a lot of his shots?

☐ **YES**   ☐ **NO**

THE BACK 9

---

10. Has this person succumbed to the *"Rocky Reaction"?* No matter how the game beats him down, is he always ready to come back for one more round?

☐ **YES**   ☐ **NO**

11. Does he show certain psychological symptoms like hallucinations; i.e., seeing great shots he never made?

☐ **YES**   ☐ **NO**

12. Or does he have memory problems; i.e., can't remember a lot of strokes he *did* take?

☐ **YES**   ☐ **NO**

13. Does he treat his clubs like a lover, embracing them with both hands no matter how many times they betray him?

☐ **YES** ☐ **NO**

14. Has this passionate player ever inflicted golf in any way, shape, or form on innocent neighbors, business associates, or in-laws? Or any minors?

☐ **YES** ☐ **NO**

15. Would you consider this person to be (the truth now)...a *"pusher"*?

☐ **YES** ☐ **NO**

16. Has your golf lover ever gone on *"bogey binges"* for days, weeks, or months at a time? Does he want to talk about it afterwards? Or does he keep it away from you, preferring to share the humiliation with friends he really needs strokes from?

☐ **YES**   ☐ **NO**

17. Has he ever abstained from playing, practicing, watching, reading, or talking about golf for more than 48 hours?

☐ **YES**   ☐ **NO**

If **"YES,"** was he conscious?

18. In all honesty, has this person spent the best years of his life—and <u>yours</u>—under the influence of a dumb little pock-marked ball?

☐ **YES**   ☐ **NO**

Now comes the really tough part. Scoring...

If You Answered "YES" To Only 1 or 2 of the 18 Questions...

You can relax.

The suspected golf addict is still pretty much a hopeless hacker, a casual swinger. Only rarely does he or she experience delusions of golfing grandeur.

The person is at a popular and fairly harmless stage we call the *"locker room golf lover."*

You have nothing to fear. (Then again, it probably wouldn't hurt to put a bowling ball in his stocking this Christmas!)

THE LOCKER ROOM GOLF LOVER

If You Answered "YES" To Any 3 Of The Questions...

That special someone has already gone from playing fast and loose to playing slow and serious. This person is at a very critical stage. They could go either way.

If 2 of the 3 **"YES"** answers were on **"The Back 9,"** I strongly advise you try easing your junior golf junkie into some diversionary activity like running with the bulls at Pamplona. Or going over Niagara Falls in a barrel. Better yet, forget the barrel. Have him tackle the Falls in his golf bag!

TRY EASING YOUR GOLF LOVER INTO SOME DIVERSIONARY ACTIVITY...

If You Answered "YES" To 4 Or More Of The Questions...

That person you suspect has indeed strayed from the straight and narrow once too often. The die has been cast. The libido of the links has taken possession of the soul!

You are living with a hard-core ball beater.
An over-heated swinger.
A golf ball junkie.
A passionate player par excellence!
In a word...a Golfaholic!

Go ahead. Have a good cry. You've earned it. You have taken the first step. A lot of people never get this far. You're entitled to let it out.

Now that you know the truth, you must face it with courage. And a positive, productive course of action!

IN A WORD...A GOLFAHOLIC!

BETWEEN NINES

On his 75th birthday a daughter asked her father how much longer he wanted to live.

"Oh another 10, 15 years would be nice..." he replied. "Unless I can't play golf. Then just go ahead an shoot me. And you better make it a hole in one!"

Dreams die hard for the real golfaholic.

PART II:

SURVIVAL OF THE FITTEST!

For those of you who have read this far because of someone near and dear you suspect as not playing with a full set of clubs, the rest of this book may offer the one chance you'll have to understand, forgive, and yes, even extract some sweet penance from the philandering passionate player in your life.

Trust me. Have I lied to you yet?

WHAT YOU MUST NOT DO...

What you must not do is expect your golfaholic to give it up. That's right.

Don't even entertain the thought. It is just not going to happen. By hoping and praying and thinking up all kinds of ways to pry your golf addict away from his playtime, you are only driving him deeper into the rough. Keep it up and suffer the consequences. The woods are full of golfaholics who have gone after errant shots only to lose their balls forever.

With that in mind, read what I am about to tell you slowly, carefully, until it is ingrained in every fibre of your being.

THERE IS NO CURE FOR YOUR GOLFAHOLIC'S BALL-BEATING OBSESSION.

No cure!
Not ever.
None.
No way.
Not in this life or the next!!
Am I making myself clear?
Good.

...LUNCHTIME QUICKIES WITH HIS LATEST MISTRESS — A NEW PUTTER!

I know this comes as a terrible blow to most of you, but you have to face facts.

A true golfaholic is sentenced to life. Which means that you, dear reader, are equally sentenced to life putting up with golf horror stories, terrible jokes; day after day of lunchtime quickies with his latest mistress—a new putter; vacations sacrificed to the eternal search for new and dangerous fairways to conquer; and weekends devoted to the physically and morally handicapped— the rest of his regular foursome.

But don't give up heart and hope. All is not lost.

While there is no known cure* (or unknown cure for that matter—at least that we know of), there are ways to make the best of life with a golfaholic. And perhaps even...take advantage of it!

*All right. There is one cure. The procedure is so risky that it is only suggested as an absolute last resort. Don't even think about it right now. We'll get to it soon enough. When you're ready.

CASE HISTORY NO. 12568418
Houston, Texas

"Shirley, my wife, has gone to at least 18 different pros in 15 states for help.

"She plays every day. We were celebrating her grandmother's 90th birthday when her eyes got all teary and she whispered in my ear, 'I've got it...I've got it!' Then rushed out of the house with her clubs.

"It's getting impossible to take her anywhere socially. If anyone even offers coffee or tea, her nostrils flare and her lower lip quivers.

'Tee?? You've got a tee time?! When? Where? My clubs are in the car!!'

"Underneath her sweet exterior lurks a wild golf animal ready to spring into her golf cart, which has an unlisted mobile phone.

"At this point I think I better start interviewing for a surrogate grieving wife for my funeral. It's not that I expect to go soon, but whenever it happens, Shirley will be on the golf course. With a little luck, we can schedule the service between the front and back nine. If we make it quick, Shirley might not even lose her turn. My wife has never let anyone play through."

How to talk to your golfaholic

Yes, I know you have tried. The problem is your words of wisdom about his ball-beating obsession don't connect for him. You have to carefully select words and images he can easily understand in his condition.

You have to sprinkle the conversation with words and phrases that are going to keep his mind from wandering, hold his attention, keep him from getting restless.

You will get much farther if you can speak the same language as your golfaholic; communicate on his level of awareness.

Learn to use words and phrases like...
- *Down the middle*
- *On the sweet spot*
- *Long knocker*
- *Big stick*
- *Scratch player*
- *Stiff*
- *Hole high*

These are good words, positive phrases, completely non-threatening. Used liberally in any conversation they are sure to bring a smile to your golfaholic's face.

**YOU'LL GET MUCH FARTHER IF YOU CAN SPEAK
THE SAME LANGUAGE AS YOUR GOLFAHOLIC**

The fact that such words might also have some sexual connotation only make them easier for him to understand.

NAUGHTY WORDS

There are also some nasty phrases and naughty words that you should never use under any circumstances:

Words like...
- *Slice*
- *Hook*
- *Fat*
- *Chili dip*
- *Whiff*
- *Double bogey*
- *Rough*
- *Shank*
- *Sudden death*

For example, tell a golf lover to *"take a whiff"* of your homemade soup and he's going to hate it.

But tell him the soup is sure to *"hit his sweet spot"* and he'll lap it up like your Schnauzer.

A word to the wise. Under no circumstances serve *"chili dip"* at a party. He'll *"double bogey"* it for sure and head for the port-a-potty.

And never, ever offer him a *"slice"* of lamb *"shank."* It's bound to be too *"fat"* or just plain *"rough."* If he isn't thinking and does take a bite, he's sure to *"choke"* on it, maybe even ruin the whole dinner party with *"sudden death."*

Before you let matters get that far, it's time to take *"a grass roots"* perspective. Simply, which would you rather have?

Your golfaholic on the course looking down at the grass, or six feet under looking up at the roots?

Don't be so quick to answer!

You may change your mind before we're through here.

Then again...

CASE HISTORY NO. 00000001
Fargo, North Dakota

"My boss has a golfing problem. He says his wife, Ethel, doesn't understand him—which is not surprising since her name is Gertrude. His putter is Ethel.

"He says they are both impossible to live with, except Gertrude doesn't miss from two feet. Which is why he hangs on to Ethel who at least doesn't hit back.

"He's played for five years to get good enough to be called a duffer.

"In the three years I've worked for him, I've listened to exactly 4,629 excuses for his lousy shots. Tomorrow I'll hear a 105 or 110 more—if he's had a good day.

"Every other week he swears he's going to give up the game, then says as long as he's going to quit, he might as well get in one more round.

"Last Christmas I almost made a terrible mistake. I bought him one of those gadgets to find the sweetspot on his balls.

"The next day he begged me to marry him. So did his wife."

A MAN, A WOMAN, AND A BAG OF CLUBS

It has been said that you can always tell how a man treats a woman by the way he drives a car. (I think it was my wife who said it after I got a speeding ticket.)

It is certainly true that dedicated golf lovers treat their clubs with at least the care they give the other love of their life.

For example, at Christmas the golfaholic will surprise the loves of his life with beautiful clothes:
For you, a genuine imitation muscrat coat.
For his precious persimmon woods, mink headcovers!

And then we have exciting evenings on the town:
You get cocktails and dinner at the Doggie Diner drive-thru express window, so he won't be late for your front row seats to the opening night of a workshop on "Club Refinishing Because You Care."

And, of course, we can't forget those spur of the moment vacations to fantasy lands:
For you, a weekend at the Hallelujah Hollywood Motel—Hourly Rates—Pets Allowed.
For the bag of clubs, an all expenses paid week in Hawaii!

Now while the above is certainly par for the course for many golfaholics, that doesn't mean it has to be par for your course.

As you will discover very soon, there are ways to take these behavioral patterns and twist them to your own advantage and profit!

CASE HISTORY NO. 46738269
Miami Beach, Florida

"I confess! I am a golfaholic. My wife is a golf widow. Our son is a golf orphan. Worst of all, I have become a 'pusher.'

"I've been inflicting golf on innocent people for the last two years. The last friend I got 'hooked' just sold his house and bought a lot on a golf course. Chester's wife and three little girls have moved in with her parents until Chester can afford to build a house on the lot.

"Chester is living with us right now. My wife says she has never seen me happier. She's right. In fact, just before our tenth wedding anniversary, I won a vacation for two to Myrtle Beach! It was like a dream come true.

"I hope my wife won't mind if we celebrate our anniversary after Chester and I get back."

**YEAH...THERE'S NOTHING LIKE
HAVING A PLACE ON THE GOLF COURSE!**

GETTING THROUGH THE WEEK WITH YOUR OVERHEATED SWINGER

The veteran golfaholic has found many ways to make it through the week until his Saturday game.

Business meetings scheduled over a bucket of balls at a local driving range are easily managed.

Mid-week fixes with friends have been going on for years.

Do not make the mistake of questioning your golf lover about these obvious ploys or you may find yourself in the following conversation:

"Why should you play all day and have all the fun while I slave away keeping the bills paid, the house clean, the kids fed..."

And he says, "All right. So take my clubs, go to the range, hit a few balls and tell me what you think."

You do. "Why that's the stupidest, dumbest, most ridiculous waste of time...How can you stand to play it?"

"You see. And all these years you thought I was having a good time!"

WHAT TO DO ABOUT WEEKENDS

Let's be real honest. At least one day of the weekend is going to be totally shot. Probably both days.

A typical scenario usually goes something like this:

Up at 2:30 A.M., dressed and out to the course where he waits in line with other addicts to secure an appointment for next weekends fix. Then back to the car where he grabs some shut-eye until his 6:30 A.M. starting time. Then 18 frustrating holes with his regular foursome of hard-core sand-baggers.

Then lunch, polish dogs, beer, and a couple of candy bars for energy to get through the card game in the lounge. Then lose a few more dollars on the putting green to a 12 year old hustler.

Then into the 19th hole to watch the pros on television and give advice as to what's wrong with Nicklaus' short game. Then out to the practice tee so he won't forget what it feels like to hit one out of 50 balls on the clubface.

He arrives home in no mood for your smiling face and the romantic evening you've planned.

Hell, how can he feel romantic when his first love, his pitching wedge, has left him cold!

Of course there are a hundred variations on this weekend scenario, but in every case, no matter how the details may vary, the results are always the same:

A frustrated, grumpy, heart-broken blob of protoplasm comes dragging in the door mumbling incoherently, and somehow you have got to get him showered and dressed like a real person and functioning enough to be your escort for the opera or ballet, or worse, an evening alone together.

Then there are those rare occasions when the golfing gods have looked kindly upon his mighty labors, and he will arrive home in such a state of euphoria and self satisfaction that you and everyone you come into contact with that night will be subjected to a slow and agonizing replay of every shot on every hole, not to mention every nuance of his mental and physical mastery over the game.

So what do you do about weekends and plans you've made for the evening?

About the best you can hope for is to see a wretched blob come blubbering in the door. By now you know how to handle that.

The only thing you really have to worry about is when a great laughing, singing, alls-right-with-the-world bouncing bubble returns from battle and scares the hell out of you!

You don't know this person. He reminds you of someone you once knew...before you got married. *Before golf!*

You're in the Twilight Zone...

...THOSE RARE OCCASIONS WHEN THE GOLFING GODS
HAVE LOOKED KINDLY UPON HIS MIGHTY LABORS...

How to Survive Vacations

Now this is tough. Living with a golfaholic and not expecting the person to play on his or her vacation is not being very realistic to the nature of the addiction.

Since there is no way you are going to get your golfaholic to agree to a vacation at any place that doesn't have a golf course, you have to make sure the place has a lot more than just a golf course.

Fortunately, there are now so many golfaholics running amok all over the world that many wonderful vacation spots not only offer the golf addict the challenge of new, exotic fairways to conquer, but also provide a host of other activities for real people.

Vacation at one of these places and with any luck you won't see or have to talk to your golfaholic until you pack your bags to leave!

Better yet, why risk it? Why not send your golf animal into the mountains or out to the desert by himself while you take a cruise on the Love Boat. You may even have a shipboard romance. And you'll be completely safe. Golfaholics always play away from the water.

THE CHALLENGE OF NEW, EXOTIC FAIRWAYS TO CONQUER

THE HORROR OF HOLIDAYS

When it comes to holidays, the golfaholic more than anyone, knows the real meaning of Thanksgiving, Easter, and Christmas.

All the hopeless hackers, casual swingers and the like will dutifully spend the day with family and friends celebrating, while he recognizes what is really meaningful about the day...

A golf course pure and free from those less than devout practitioners; a golf course where he can worship in the presence of only those true disciples who feel the same as he does about the game.

In other words, Christmas and Thanksgiving are for shooting birdies—even at the risk of being a turkey to the rest of the family.

Now is the WINTER OF OUR DISCONTENT...

Shakespeare must have been a golfaholic. How else could he have written such a line as the title of this chapter.

Yes, every winter thousands of golfaholics suffer the pain and anguish of going *"Cold Bogey."*

This period is even harder on you. In order to survive the long winter, you have to learn how to play with your golf lover.

Surprise him. Set up a miniature golf course through the house so he has a place to play, then invite his golfing buddies over to play with him.

Or why not indulge his golf fantasies? Go all the way. Buy him the latest Jan Stephenson Calendar and hang it over the bed!

Why do all this?

Because your golfaholic needs all the T.L.C. he can get in this most critical time of need.

Because to a real golf addict a week without a waggle is like a day without sunshine.

But primarily because tender loving care and understanding carefully invested in your golfaholic during the winter can be commodities of great value on the **Guilt Exchange** the rest of the year.

Yes, your patience is about to be rewarded!

CASHING IN ON YOUR GOLFAHOLIC

Keeping your golfaholic happy during the long winter months can be one of the best investments you'll ever make.

If handled properly, your golfaholic will be so overcome by your thoughtfulness that he won't think twice when you suggest the following rate of exchange.

GOLFAHOLIC GETS:

An afternoon of video cassettes of the U.S. Open, the British Open, and the Masters with three golf junkie friends. Cold cuts and beer available. Self-serve.

EXCHANGE RATE:

You get an afternoon at Bloomingdales, Saks Fifth Avenue, and Nieman Marcus with three girlfriends who know how to make it and spend it.

A leisurely lunch at the "in" new bistro where the way the handsome young waiter looks at you makes you feel like a wanted woman. You order wine, watercress, and the waiter for dessert.

GOLFAHOLIC GETS:

One Saturday round, 18 holes—winter rules—across the living room, around the den, through your bedroom and into the kitchen with his regular foursome.

You caddie, keep all scores, provide tee prizes, awards, and serve lunch with hot entree, cold potatoes, jello salad, and choice of beverage.

EXCHANGE RATE:

You get a week at the Golden Door. You get pampered and catered to, enjoy massages, herbal wraps, and mud baths.

You return home rejuvinated, reborn, and ready to face your golfaholic and not flinch at his blinding polyester plaid pants.

GOLFAHOLIC GETS:

A fantasy night with Jan Stephenson. You promise not to laugh at his fore-play.

EXCHANGE RATE:

You get a real night at Chippendales. One of the liberated ladies with you knows one of the hard bodies and sets you up after the show.

The young hunk thinks you're a real hunkette. He takes you to his pad. You are afraid, but you have to ask. Does he like to...that 4-letter world? *"Golf?... What's that?"* he answers innocently.

This guy really knows how to score.

Obviously the above are only suggested rates of exchange.

Of course when golf season blossoms once again in the spring, you instigate a much simpler game plan...

Whatever he spends on green fees, lessons, golf hardware, software, and underwear, you spend an equal amount on shopping, the stock market, precious metals, diamonds, limos and lobster!

It'll be tough keeping up with him, but do the best you can.

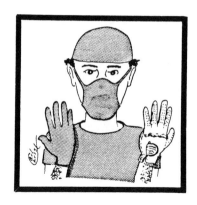

CASE HISTORY NO. 7326732
Detroit, Michigan

"It's true. I'm a golf junkie. Anytime. Anyplace. Any danger! Why? Because they are out there. Luscious golf courses. Seductive creatures that beckon with their earthy charms.

"From high flying balls in the Bolivian Andes to frozen balls near the Arctic Circle, my lust has driven me. There aren't many men who can say they have 4-putted in five Continents!

"I can never get enough. I've got to have a club in my hand at least three or four times a day, even when I'm working. In the O.R. last week they said I tried to remove a gall bladder with a 9-iron.

"I don't remember exactly what happened, but I think I bogeyed the hole. Probably needed more club."

SCALPEL, FORCEPS... 9-IRON!

ITS ALL IN THE MIND

The game of golf does strange things to the minds of its more committed zealots.

The rabid golfaholic cannot just walk away after having been abjectly defeated by an insignificantly pock-marked ball over which, by all rights, he or she should have control.

In the mind of the true golf junkie, the solution is always more—one more shot, one more round, more paraphernalia, more lessons, always more of that four letter word, Fore!

Unfortunately, rather than being an uplifting experience, the game often becomes nothing less than bondage, teasing, and taunting its devotees; insinuating itself into the soul; raising expectations of heart stopping pleasures, leading its practitioners to the very brink of ecstasy before dropping them cold, frustrated and hungering for one last whack at it.

When this happens and your golfer comes home miserable, you might suggest he try to think of the game more in the spirit the Scots intended. More like a grand adventure rather than something he has to be in control of and master.

In other words, there are many paths from the 1st tee to the 18th green. The road less traveled may be the most exciting one of all!

It doesn't matter what he shoots, but the manner in which he goes about it. That's where the fun is!

If his eyes begin to glow and he begins to drool and growl, you might remind him that if profanity had any influence on the flight of his ball, he'd play the game far better than he does.

Now that you have got his attention, suggest that if he can only find it in his spiked soul to somehow laugh at his warped dedication to such a diabolical game, then the traps and hazards of the real world will be an easy par.

If he laughs at the idea, you may have found an opening. But make sure it's laughter and not hysteria—in which case you may want to find a bunker to hide in.

LONG TERM PROGNOSIS

Before you can even think long term, you have to get your golfaholic past the stage of denial.

He has to once and for all *"come out of the locker room"* about his magnificent obsession.

You have to convince him that confession is not only good for the soul, it is even better for his golf swing!

Of course it would be nice if he could learn to occasionally laugh at his handicap.

Short of that, I sincerely hope that with help from this book, you will now be able to find it in your heart to understand, forgive and, yes, even encourage the passionate player in your life in his impossible dream to conquer the dimpled demon within.

I have tried to show you ways to make living with a golfaholic a little more bearable.

There is, however, one course of action I have purposely left to last.

Why?

Because it is the most potent medication I can prescribe and can be life threatening.

Read on at your own risk. Remember, I warned you.

HERE IT IS:

Ask your golfaholic to give you lessons. Spend hours on the driving range with him. Don't accept lessons from anyone else. You want to learn from your golfaholic. Make him teach you everything he knows about the game.

Spend whole weekends on the course at his side. Follow him into the rough. Find his balls for him. On the green tell him which way his putts break.

Take advantage of all his years of playing the game.

Take the game as seriously as he does. As miserable as he can be to live with, you can be even more miserable after a bad round.

Why?

Because by watching his *every* move, you'll learn precisely what *not* to do and *see* exactly how *not* to do it!

I know we're dealing with risky business here. Two things can happen:

One: He's willing to do anything to get you off the course, including suggesting a weekend away without your clubs... or his! You agree, but not until he begs for it. Victory, at last!

Two: You get hooked on the game, learn to play it much better than he ever did and thrash him soundly in front of his friends.

He is mortified and quits in complete despair. Worse, he now has to live with you, a golfaholic convert! You're the worst kind!

Swingers like you show no mercy.

The poor guy doesn't know what he's in for. Why not give the guy a break? Loan him this book...

I think he's going to need it!

**...BY WATCHING HIS EVERY MOVE,
YOU'LL LEARN PRECISELY WHAT *NOT* TO DO**

YES, THERE REALLY IS A GOLFAHOLICS ANONYMOUS®

We have pretty well established that nearly all golfers share the following traits:

That they will do anything to hit the ball straighter, higher, longer...

And buy any new piece of hardware, software, or underwear that promises to accomplish the above.

Yet there are still going to be far more days when the ball goes where it damn well pleases rather than where the golfer pleases.

Simply, golfers are going to be frustrated, humbled, and humiliated by the maddening game (if it is a game at all), far more than they will ever be satisfied and fulfilled.

Now while most golfers share in the above, what they don't share is a refuge, a place where they can bare their spiked souls, share their tales of woe about the game in an atmosphere of understanding and forgiveness.

You certainly don't want to hear anymore about it!

Well, at last there is such a haven for the severly *"handicapped."* An organization whose principles hard-core ball-beaters can espouse; whose goals they can adopt without fear or shame. A fellowship that die-hard golf lovers can identify with.

It is called **Golfaholics Anonymous.**

Golfaholics Anonymous offers no cure and preaches no reform. A real golfaholic is sentenced to life!

But you already knew that.

Golfaholics Anonymous believes that golfaholics must first own up to their magnificent obsession before they can truly begin to enjoy the guilt!

Members of Golfaholics Anonymous eventually learn that having a good sense of humor about the maddening game helps them to relax and play to the best of their abilities rather than the worst.

After all, the game is hard enough that if you can't laugh at your "handicap," it surely will drive you nuts. Both of you!

So, after you try everything suggested in this book, if your golf animal is still impossible to live with, you might consider turning the problem over to *"professional help."*

Golfaholics Anonymous won't cure your golfer of his ball-beating dependency, but it will help him smile through his tears.

And yours.

THE UNREACHABLE PAR

Real golfaholics are like Don Quixote tilting at flagsticks...

To dream the impossible dream
To beat the unbeatable game
To try when you're topping and shanking
To not take in vain the Lord's name

To drive where the Pros dare not go
To watch and not croak from the poke
To bear the unbearable O.B.
To putt and not choke from the stroke

This is my quest
To swing at that ball
To slice and to hook it
I'll swing til I fall

To fight for a three, a deuce or an ace!
To be willing to duff through the rough
Yes, this must be the place

To hit high and wide in the woods
To play from unplayable junk
To try when your arms are too weary
To blast from a bottomless bunk

This is my quest
To follow that ball
Wherever it leads me
I'll crawl proud and tall

To go for that bird, an eagle I'd take
I'll admit that I hit my best balls
When I tripped on a rake!

And I know
If I'll only be true
To this glorious quest
That my clubs
Will lie peaceful and calm
When we par in the rest

And the game will be better for this
That one man labeled crazed and bizarre
Still strove with his mashie and niblick
To reach the unreachable par!!

THE UNREACHABLE PAR

OTHER GOLF BOOKS BY MARK OMAN

Portrait Of A Golfaholic
Illustrated by Gary Patterson
(96 pages—30 illustrations) ISBN 0-8092-5335-6 $6.95

The bible of Golfaholics Anonymous. A look into the wide world of golfaholism.

"A great gift to the guy in your foursome who is always pressing for 6 A.M. tee times...Every sinner loves company."
Los Angeles Times

The Sensuous Golfer — *How To Play THE GAME...On The Course And Off!!*
Illustrated by Tom Nix
(72 pages—32 illustrations) ISBN 0-917346-01-7 $6.95

The perfect gift for everyone's favorite sensuous golfer—and would-be sensuous golfer!

★ ★ ★ ★ ★

The above books are available at golf course pro shops, better bookstores, and fine gift shops.

To order an autographed copy of these books, or find out more about a Lifetime Membership in **Golfaholics Anonymous,** please write to:

GOLFAHOLICS ANONYMOUS®
P.O. Box 222357B Carmel, CA 93922

To cover shipping of book orders, please include $1.00 for first book and 50ᶜ for each additional book. CA residents please add 6% sales tax.